HOW TO GROW CARE MANAGE AND USE CALENDULA FOR PROFIT

A Comprehensive Guide To Cultivating, Nurturing, And Expert Tips Strategies FOR Commercializing Calendula Flowers For Profit

LARRY NANCY

This book "How to Grow, Care, Manage, and Use Calendula for Profit" is a complete guide that is very helpful for anyone who wants to grow calendula for personal or business reasons.

The book covers many topics about calendula, from how to grow it to how to market it.

The first few chapters give a solid background by talking about the history, different types, and traditional uses of calendula. They also focus on the possible market and profitability, giving readers an idea of whether or not growing calendula is a good business idea.

The book goes beyond simple growing instructions and talks about all the wonderful things calendula can do for you. From its healing and medicinal properties to its uses in skin care products and food, readers get a full picture of this useful plant.

This book's useful tips on how to set up and run a successful calendula farm are some of its best features.

These tips cover important things like picking the right location, getting the dirt ready, and picking the right types of calendula plants for different climates and times of the year.

The book walks readers through the whole process of growing plants, from finding good seeds to germination methods, transplanting, and ongoing care. It also talks about important aspects of plant maintenance, such as how-to water, fertilize, and get rid of pests.

Another great thing is that it focuses on gathering and handling after harvesting. This includes when and how to harvest, as well as important steps for drying, storing, and making sure of the quality of the calendula product.

The guide goes one step further by talking about how to make value-added products like infused oils, extracts, herbal teas, and skin care products.

This not only makes calendula more profitable, but it also gives readers new ideas.

The last few parts of the book are all about important business topics, like marketing strategies, legal and regulatory issues, and how to grow a calendula business so that it will be successful and last for a long time.

In essence, "How to Grow, Care, Manage, and Use Calendula for Profit" is not just a gardening book; it is also a complete business guide that teaches readers how to not only grow calendula successfully but also make money from it. This book is helpful for both new and experienced growers because it shows them how to make calendula cultivation a profitable business.

CHAPTER ONE
WHAT YOU NEED TO KNOW ABOUT CALENDULA

Scientists have named calendula, or Calendula officinalis, a beautiful and useful herb that has gained popularity for both its decorative and healing properties. To understand calendula and its different types, it is important to know what it looks like. Calendula comes from the Asteraceae family and has bright orange or yellow flowers with unique ray and disc florets. The plant also has strong, branched stems and lance-shaped leaves.

Historical Significance And Usages From The Past

If you look into the history of Calendula, you'll find that it has been used for many different things over many hundreds of years. This herb comes from Southern Europe and has been used for cooking, beauty, and medicine. In traditional medicine, it was praised for its ability to reduce inflammation, kill germs, and calm muscles. The Greeks and Egyptians were among the people who knew this and used it to treat a wide range of ailments.

Profitability And Possible Market

Growing calendula has a lot of potential for people who want to make money in the herbal market. The growing interest in natural remedies and health has put calendula in the spotlight, creating a strong market demand. The cosmetic industry, in particular, values calendula for its skin-soothing properties, which has led to a rise in the use of calendula extracts in skin care products.

The herbal tea market has also seen a rise.

How To Grow Calendula

If you want to grow Calendula successfully, you need to know exactly what it needs to grow. Calendula does best in well-drained, moderately fertile soil and likes to be in the sun.

To grow it, you can either plant the seeds directly in the ground or start seedlings indoors and move them outside later. Make sure there is enough space between plants to keep air flowing and keep diseases away. Regularly watering, especially

Taking Care Of Calendula

Effective care is essential for keeping Calendula plants healthy and producing lots of flowers. The herb is pretty low-maintenance, but paying attention to certain things can have a big effect on its overall health. For example, it's important to water it regularly and avoid waterlogging to avoid root rot and fungal diseases. Mulching around the plants' bases helps keep the soil moist and stops weeds from growing. Finally, it's important to check for pests like aphids and spider mites regularly.

Taking Care Of Calendula Plants

Strategic planning, attention to detail, and being proactive in solving problems are all important parts of running a Calendula cultivation business. Setting a well-thought-out planting schedule lets farmers take advantage of seasonal trends and market demands. Integrated pest management methods, like companion planting or introducing beneficial insects, help make cultivation sustainable and eco-friendly. Efficient harvesting methods, like using sharp,

Making Money With Calendula

Calendula can be used in many ways besides growing it. For example, cosmetics like creams, lotions, and balms contain calendula extracts, which can be used to make them more profitable. Making artisanal soaps or bath products with calendula added to them can also add value to the products. In the food industry, dried calendula petals can be added to teas and infusions or used as a tasty topping for salads and desserts.

CHAPTER TWO
WHAT CALENDULA CAN DO FOR YOU

Calendula is a colorful and useful growing plant that has many useful properties that make it a good choice for people who want to grow plants for profit. These useful properties can be used in many areas, such as medicine, beauty products, and food.

Properties That Make It Useful For Medicine And Health

Calendula has many health benefits that have been known and used for hundreds of years. The plant has chemicals in it like flavonoids, saponins, and triterpenoids that help it heal wounds by reducing inflammation and promoting tissue growth. Calendula extracts have also been used for centuries to treat skin conditions.

Calendula has been shown to help with digestive problems because it is a mild laxative.

Its antimicrobial properties suggest that it can fight infections both internally and externally. Calendula has also shown promise in treating conditions like ulcers and gastrointestinal discomfort. As the need for natural remedies grows, growers can make a lot of money by using calendula in medicinal ways.

Using Calendula In Skin Care Products

For its ability to soothe and rejuvenate skin, calendula has become popular in the skin care industry. The plant's extracts, which are usually taken from its bright orange or yellow petals, are used in many skin care products. Creams, lotions, and ointments that contain calendula are known to be good for your skin. Calendula's anti-inflammatory properties make it a great choice for products that target conditions.

Calendula is used to treat acne and other skin problems because it is naturally antiseptic and antimicrobial. It is also gentle, which makes it appealing to people who want botanical alternatives to synthetic skincare ingredients.

To take advantage of this demand, growers can promote calendula as a key ingredient in the creation of high-quality, natural skincare products, thereby tapping into the growing market for these products.

How To Use It In Cooking And How Healthy It Is

Calendula is useful for more than just medicine and skin care. The petals, which have a mild, slightly peppery flavor, can be added to salads, soups, and other dishes. Their bright color makes them look better and adds nutritional value.

Carotenoids, which are found in calendula petals, are powerful antioxidants that help protect eyesight and boost the immune system.

Using calendula in cooking makes these health benefits more enjoyable and tastier for customers.

 As people become more interested in healthy and aesthetically pleasing foods, using calendula in cooking can be a unique selling point for growers who want to sell more of their crops.

People who want to make money from calendula can do so in several ways. Whether they focus on the plant's medicinal uses, skin benefits, or culinary uses, they need to know all of its different qualities to grow and sell it successfully.

By strategically placing calendula in these different markets, growers can not only take advantage of its economic potential but also make a lot of money from it.

CHAPTER THREE
MAKING PLANS FOR YOUR CALENDULA FARM

If you want to grow calendula for profit, you need to plan everything out very carefully. One of the first things you need to do is choose a site and prepare the soil. The site you choose should have the best conditions for calendula growth. Calendula does best in well-drained soil with a slightly acidic to neutral pH. It also needs to get enough sunlight, so you need to choose a spot that gets full or partial sunlight. To prepare the soil, you have to till it.

Choosing the right calendula varieties is an important part of planning. Different cultivars have different flower shapes, sizes, and colors. Knowing what the market wants and needs helps you choose varieties that meet those needs. You should also think about things like bloom time and disease resistance.

Having a wide range of calendula varieties can meet the needs of different customers and make your crop more durable.

Climate and seasonal factors are important for growing calendula successfully. Calendula can grow in a variety of climates, but it does best in mild conditions. Knowing the climate and seasons of the chosen location helps with planning when to plant and harvest. It's important to keep in mind frost dates and temperature changes to protect the delicate calendula flowers. In places with distinct seasons, planting times need to be changed.

Choosing A Site And Getting The Soil Ready

Site selection and soil preparation are the first steps to starting a successful calendula farm. The chosen site should have good conditions for calendula growth, like full or partial sun. Well-drained soil with a slightly acidic to neutral pH range is also ideal for growing calendula. A soil test can help you figure out the soil's nutrient composition and pH, which includes targ

Soil preparation includes a few important steps. First, the land should be cleared of trash and weeds to make a good place to grow plants. Next, the soil should be worked to make it more porous so roots can reach deeper into it. Finally, organic matter like compost or well-rotted manure should be added to add nutrients and improve the structure of the soil. This step is very important to make sure the soil stays moist without getting too wet.

How To Pick The Right Kinds Of Calendula

The choice of calendula varieties is a big deal that affects the success of a calendula farm. Calendula cultivars have different flower colors, sizes, and shapes, so they can meet the needs of a wide range of customers. Knowing your target market and what they want is important for making smart choices when choosing varieties. Some varieties may be more popular in certain areas or markets, so giving variety selection some thought is important.

Another important thing to think about is when the flowers will bloom. If farmers choose varieties with staggered bloom times, they can extend the harvest period and have a steadier supply of calendula flowers. Disease resistance is also important because it can affect the crop's overall health and productivity. Farmers should try to get a balanced mix of varieties that not only meet market needs but also resist diseases and pests.

Climate And Seasonal Factors To Think About

As a versatile plant, calendula can grow in a wide range of climates. However, it is important to know the specific climate and seasonal patterns of the chosen location to grow it successfully. Calendula does best in temperate climates, and care should be taken to ensure that it grows at its best during each season. In colder climates, knowing when the plants are most likely to be damaged by frost is especially important.

Schedules for planting and harvesting should be in line with the local climate and seasons. In places with clear seasons, planning when to plant ensures a steady supply of calendula flowers. Calendula blooms best in cooler temperatures, so it can be grown in early spring and late fall. By carefully choosing when to plant and harvest, farmers can get the most out of their calendula crop in terms of yield and quality.

Additionally, climate affects how water is managed. Calendula needs consistent moisture, so farmers should come up with irrigation plans that work with the local climate. In hotter and drier areas, extra irrigation may be needed to make sure the plants grow and produce flowers at their best. Overall, knowing the climate and seasonal changes of the chosen location is essential for growing calendula for profit.

CHAPTER FOUR
HOW TO GROW CALENDULA FROM SEEDS

Growing calendula for profit is possible because it has beautiful flowers and healing properties.

The first thing you need to do is get high-quality seeds. Seed sourcing is an important part of growing calendula for profit; choose reputable suppliers that are known for providing seeds with a high germination rate and genetic purity.

It is also important to make sure the seeds are free of any contaminants.

Techniques for germination are very important for starting the growth cycle. Calendula seeds usually do well when planted directly in prepared soil, but you can also use other methods, such as starting seeds indoors. Using a seed-starting mix that helps seeds drain and a controlled environment with the right temperature and moisture levels can greatly improve germination rates.

Be patient at this stage, as calendula seeds may take up to two weeks to sprout.

Once the seeds have sprouted, they need to be moved and cared for very carefully. Calendula plants do best in slightly acidic to neutral soil. Transplant seedlings when they have two true leaves, making sure they are spaced out enough to grow properly. Watering regularly is important, but be careful not to let the soil become too wet, as this can cause root rot. Mulching around the plants helps keep the soil moist and keeps weeds away.

How To Take Care Of And Grow Calendula

To get the best yield and quality from calendula, it needs careful care and management throughout the growing season. Pests and diseases need to be checked regularly so that problems can be dealt with quickly. Planting insect-repelling herbs next to the calendula can help keep them away naturally, so you don't have to use chemicals. Pruning off spent flowers keeps them blooming and stops them from self-seeding, which keeps the desired genet.

For calendula to get the nutrients it needs, it needs to be fertilized properly. A balanced fertilizer with a slightly higher phosphorus content helps flowers grow. Organic options, like compost or well-rotted manure, improve soil fertility and long-term sustainability. Be careful not to over-fertilize, though, because too many nutrients can cause plants to grow leggy and produce fewer flowers.

Calendulas are tough and can survive drought, but they need to be watered regularly, especially during dry spells, to make sure they grow and flower at their best. Mulching helps plants keep water in, keeps weeds down, and keeps the soil at a comfortable temperature.

When it comes to harvesting calendula, timing is very important. The flowers should be picked when they are fully open but before they start to wilt. To keep the medicinal properties of the flowers, they should be dried properly, such as by air drying in a cool, well-ventilated area.

Making Money With Calendula

Calendula is a valuable commodity for making money because it can be used in many different fields, such as medicine, food, and cosmetics.

In the cosmetics industry, calendula extracts are used in skin care products because they soothe and reduce inflammation. For example, you can make money by partnering with local cosmetic manufacturers or making your cosmetics.

There are many business opportunities in the medicinal market. Calendula is known for its ability to kill germs and reduce inflammation. Making tinctures, salves, or oils to sell in health stores or directly to people who want natural remedies can be a profitable business. Getting certified for organic or sustainable practices may also help your products sell better.

Although not as common, calendula petals can also be used in cooking. They can be used to add color to salads, soups, or desserts, which could mean working with chefs or getting into the gourmet food market. In this niche, it's important to follow food safety rules and best practices.

Setting up an online presence through a website or social media is an important part of marketing Calendula products. Educating content about how to grow calendula, its benefits, and creative ways to use it can bring in customers. Making connections with local markets, health stores, and herbalists can also help you make sales.

Calendula needs to be carefully chosen as seeds, carefully cared for and managed, and strategically marketed to be grown and used for profit. By understanding the details of each step in the process, individuals can not only grow a successful calendula crop but also reach a wide range of markets, contributing to a successful and long-lasting business.

CHAPTER FIVE
HOW TO TAKE CARE OF A CALENDULA PLANT

Calendula is a colorful and useful herbaceous plant that has become popular for both its beauty and its many medical and culinary uses. If you want to grow calendula for profit, you need to learn how to take good care of it. Watering and irrigation are very important for making sure the plant grows and develops properly. Calendula does best in well-drained soil, so keeping the soil moist is very important.

Fertilization and soil maintenance are very important parts of growing calendula. Plants do best in nutrient-rich soil, and adding organic matter like compost makes the soil more fertile.

A balanced fertilizer with a slightly higher phosphorus content encourages blooming.

It is best to test the soil regularly to see how much phosphorus is in it and then adjust the fertilization as needed. Mulching around calendula plants not only keeps the soil moist but also stops weeds from growing.

Taking proactive steps to control pests and diseases is important for a successful calendula business. Common pests like aphids and spider mites can be a problem, so it's best to use integrated pest management (IPM) methods. These include introducing natural predators, using insecticidal soaps, and checking plants often for signs of infestation. Diseases, especially fungal problems like powdery mildew, can be avoided by giving plants enough space between each other.

For a business to be successful, it's important to know more than just how to take care of plants. You also need to know how the market works and what customers want. Calendula can be used in many different ways, from making herbal teas to skin care products. To turn calendula cultivation into a profitable business, you need to create a brand identity, look for niche markets, and stick to quality standards.

As the growing process goes on, harvesting techniques become more important.

The right time to pick calendula flowers ensures that they are at their most useful for medicine and beauty products. Careful drying methods should be used to keep the plant's healthy compounds intact. Processing, packaging, and storing the flowers after harvest are also very important to keep the quality of the products and make sure that consumers get them in the best condition possible.

Several steps need to be taken to turn growing calendula into a profitable business.

The first is careful plant care, which includes effective watering and irrigation strategies, proper fertilization, and proactive pest and disease management. Next is market awareness, strategic branding, and careful attention to post-harvest processes. With these steps, people can fully utilize the potential of calendula cultivation for both financial gain and the good of the environment.

CHAPTER SIX
HARVESTING AND HANDLING AFTER HARVEST

Calendula is a beautiful and useful medicinal herb that needs to be carefully harvested to get the best yield and quality.

When and how it is harvested are two of the most important factors that affect its medicinal value and ability to be sold commercially.

The best time to harvest calendula is during the flowering stage when the plant's essential oil content is highest.

This usually happens in the early morning, after the dew has evaporated.

How To Dry And Store Calendula

Post-harvest care is just as important for how long calendula lasts and how well it works. The flowers must be dried quickly to stop mold growth and protect the bioactive compounds.

The best way to dry calendula is in a well-ventilated area, out of direct sunlight.

This way, the flowers keep their bright color, flavor, and medicinal properties.

Checking For Quality And Packing

For commercial calendula to be grown, strict quality control measures must be put in place during the growing and harvesting processes. Regular testing for pesticides, heavy metals, and microbial contaminants makes sure that the calendula meets regulatory standards and is safe for consumers.

Key bioactive compounds, such as flavonoids and triterpene, must also be monitored.

To grow calendula for profit, you need to know everything there is to know about the harvesting and handling that comes after.

 Careful planning of when and how to harvest, along with careful drying and storage, keeps the plant's healing properties.

Adding strict quality control measures and thoughtful packaging makes Calendula even more marketable, putting it in a premium position.

CHAPTER SEVEN
VALUE-ADDED PRODUCTS

Calendula is famous for its bright flowers and healing properties. It can be a good business opportunity for people who want to start making more valuable products. By doing more than just growing the plant, people can reach more customers and make more money. They can do this by making skincare and beauty products with calendula in them, as well as oils and extracts that contain calendula.

Making Oils And Extracts With Calendula

To make infused oils and extracts with calendula, the plant's healing properties are used on the skin and in medicine. Calendula is a valuable ingredient because it reduces inflammation and fights bacteria and fungi. To make infused oils, dried calendula flowers are soaked in carrier oils like olive or almond oil. This process, called maceration, lets the oil absorb the good compounds from the flowers.

Making Tinctures And Herbal Teas

Calendula is popular in herbal teas and tinctures because it has a mild flavor and many health benefits. To make herbal teas, dried Calendula flowers are mixed with other herbs that go well with them to make blends that are both tasty and useful. Calendula teas are liked for their soothing taste and for their ability to help with digestive problems and boost the immune system. Tinctures, on the other hand, are concentrated liquids that contain flowers.

Making Beauty And Skin Care Products

Because the beauty and cosmetics industry is always looking for natural and effective ingredients, calendula is a great plant to use in beauty and skincare products. Calendula's anti-inflammatory and antioxidant properties make it a popular ingredient in skincare products. Entrepreneurs can try making creams, lotions, and serums with calendula to treat skin problems like irritation, redness, and dryness.

By making value-added products, entrepreneurs can take Calendula cultivation beyond its traditional limits. They can use the plant's healing properties to make a wide range of products, such as infused oils and extracts, herbal teas and tinctures, and skin care and beauty products. This strategy not only increases market reach but also helps businesses stand out in a crowded market.

CHAPTER EIGHT
IS ABOUT HOW TO MARKET AND SELL CALENDULA PRODUCTS

Understanding Your Target Market Figuring out who you want to sell your calendula products to is an important part of running any business, including growing and selling them.

The type of people you want to sell your products to will depend on what they are used for.

For example, if you are selling skincare products, your target market might include people with sensitive skin or people looking for natural remedies.

Building an Online Presence In today's business world, you need to have a strong online presence. To leave a digital footprint for your calendula products, you need to make a website that is easy to use and looks good, use social media, and do e-commerce.

 A well-designed website can be a hub for information about calendula, its benefits, and the products you offer.

Sales Strategies and Distribution Channels Developing effective sales strategies and selecting appropriate distribution channels are integral components of a successful calendula business. Direct sales through online platforms, farmers' markets, and local stores can be complemented by strategic partnerships with retailers and wholesalers.

Creating product bundles or gift sets can enhance sales, attracting customers looking for value and variety. Offering promotions and discounts during peak seasons can stimulate sales and build customer loyalty.

Exploring international markets is another avenue for growth, requiring an understanding of export regulations and potential partnerships.

Maintaining a flexible approach to distribution, including both online and offline channels, ensures adaptability to evolving market trends. Regularly analyzing sales data and customer feedback allows for continuous refinement of sales strategies, optimizing for customer satisfaction and business profitability.

CHAPTER NINE
WHAT YOU NEED TO KNOW ABOUT LAWS AND REGULATIONS

If you want to grow, care for, manage, and use calendula for profit, you need to know a lot about the laws and rules that apply to the farming sector so that you can be successful.

Understanding The Rules For Farming

When growing calendula for profit, one of the most important things to do is to follow the rules about land use, water rights, and environmental issues. It is important to follow zoning laws and agricultural permits to stay out of trouble with the law. Understanding regional, national, and international agricultural policies is also important for making sure that your calendula farm is sustainable and follows the law.

Labeling and following the rules for herbal products

The right labeling and compliance of herbal products made from calendula goes beyond just growing the plant for profit. Clear product labels are important for consumers and for following the rules set by regulatory bodies. Following Good Agricultural Practices (GAP) and Good Manufacturing Practices (GMP) is important to meet industry standards. Understanding and following the labeling rules set by regulatory bodies makes sure that products are safe for consumers.

Making Sure Of Quality And Getting Certified

Quality control is very important in the whole calendula growing process, from the seed to the finished product. Getting certifications like organic or Fair Trade makes sure that the calendula is grown and processed ethically and meets the quality standards. Following these certifications makes Calendula products more marketable and gives customers confidence. Tough tests for contaminants, potency, and purity should be part of the production process.

To grow, care for, manage, and use calendula for profit, you need to know a lot about agricultural laws, follow labeling and compliance standards to the letter, and be dedicated to quality assurance and certification. This all-around approach not only makes sure you follow the law, but also builds a foundation for sustainable and ethical business practices in the herbal products industry.

CHAPTER TEN
GROWING YOUR CALENDULA BUSINESS

How To Increase Your Calendula Production

To grow and scale your business, you need to carefully evaluate your current production capacity, taking into account things like available land, resources, and labor. You should also do a thorough market analysis to find out where there is a need for calendula products and where your business could grow. Investing in advanced farming methods like hydroponics or greenhouse farming can greatly improve the quality of your products.

Partnering And Working Together

Partnerships and collaborations are very important to the success of a calendula business. Look for potential partners, like herbalists, skincare product makers, or health and wellness brands, to see if you can work together on projects that will benefit both of you. Examples of collaborative efforts include joint marketing campaigns, co-branded product development, or shared distribution channels. Forming partnerships with local farmers or suppliers can also help you find more calendulas.

Sustainability And Success Over The Long Term

For your calendula business to be successful and last for a long time, you need to look at it as a whole. Use sustainable farming methods to keep the soil fertile, use less water, and have less of an effect on the environment. Spend money on research and development to keep improving growing methods and product quality. You might also want to get certifications for organic or sustainable practices, which can help your brand's reputation and appeal to environmentalists.

CONCLUSION

Calendula needs to be grown, cared for, managed, and used in a way that makes money. To increase production, current capacities need to be evaluated, new cultivation techniques need to be used, and product varieties need to be diversified. Partnerships and collaborations are important for expanding market reach, improving product development, and building a strong industry network. Long-term success and sustainability depend on sustainable farming practices.

What Makes Difficult People Difficult?

A Guideline on How Best To Deal With Them

By: Ronald Smith

9781635012644

PUBLISHERS NOTES

Disclaimer – Speedy Publishing LLC

This publication is intended to provide helpful and informative material. It is not intended to diagnose, treat, cure, or prevent any health problem or condition, nor is intended to replace the advice of a physician. No action should be taken solely on the contents of this book. Always consult your physician or qualified health-care professional on any matters regarding your health and before adopting any suggestions in this book or drawing inferences from it.

The author and publisher specifically disclaim all responsibility for any liability, loss or risk, personal or otherwise, which is incurred as a consequence, directly or indirectly, from the use or application of any contents of this book.

Any and all product names referenced within this book are the trademarks of their respective owners. None of these owners have sponsored, authorized, endorsed, or approved this book.

Always read all information provided by the manufacturers' product labels before using their products. The author and publisher are not responsible for claims made by manufacturers.

This book was originally printed before 2014. This is an adapted reprint by Speedy Publishing LLC with newly updated content designed to help readers with much more accurate and timely information and data.

Speedy Publishing LLC

40 E Main Street, Newark, Delaware, 19711

Contact Us: 1-888-248-4521

Website: http://www.speedypublishing.co

REPRINTED Paperback Edition: 9781635012644:

Manufactured in the United States of America